T0199189

What Do You See
When You Look At Me?

Written by Valerie Love
Illustrated by Bella Elizondo

WestBow Press books may be ordered through booksellers or by contacting:

WestBow Press
A Division of Thomas Nelson & Zondervan
1663 Liberty Drive
Bloomington, IN 47403
www.westbowpress.com
844-714-3454

Interior Image Credit: Bella Elizondo

ISBN: 978-1-6642-2572-5 (sc)
ISBN: 978-1-6642-2573-2 (e)

Library of Congress Control Number: 2021904137

Print information available on the last page.

WestBow Press rev. date: 08/30/2021

WESTBOW
PRESS®
A DIVISION OF THOMAS NELSON
& ZONDERVAN

What do you see when you look at me?

Do you see a kid with soft hair or course?

Do you notice if I am tall or if I am short?

Perhaps you see the color of my skin?

Do you see that's it's just layers thin?

Does it matter to you if I am a boy that likes pink or a girl that likes blue?

Weren't all colors made for me and for you?

Shhhhh! Do you want to know a secret?

What you see about me, is me!

But wait! Don't stop there,
You're nearly there!
If I share, I hope you will care.

To really see me, you
will need to look deep!
That's where you'll find
that I am truly unique.

You see...Deep in my heart
is the place that I keep all
my loves and my dreams.

Those are the things that make me really me.

I know they are there
but can you see?

And, if at all possible, I'd step out of my skin, just to help show you what a powerful person lives here within.

Do you see a kid with dreams to sing, play guitar, help animals get better or just have a passion to keep the earth clean?

Maybe at just a glance
it's hard to see, but don't
forget those kinds of
things are living in me.

Matter of fact, I may
be small, called a child
and act kinda wild.

Yet, hidden in this shell,
of something small, I will
eventually grow tall.

And no matter my race, or the color, I will discover that in me is a key to our world's future.

But, can you see?

Now that you know where to look, remember that you may see a kid with a whole lot of features, but my heart is asking for you to look deeper.

So, seeing me in a different light, I hope you will stand up and fight, by believing in the dreams of us little ones, brown, red, tan, black or white.

Remember that we hold a right to be looked at with love and to be handled as if given as gifts from above.

Now, what do you see
when you look at me?

About the Author

Valerie Love is a mom of three energetic kids is married to her husband Manny. She has almost attained her Bachelor's degree in Education from Texas State University and is looking forward to becoming an elementary teacher. She loves nature, diversity, people, her supportive family and church family and especially loves inspiring kids to get creative.

Bella Elizondo, the Illustrator, is Valerie's 8 year-old daughter. This nature-girl enjoys taking care of her 6 chickens, 2 parakeets, 3 cats and 2 bunnies. Mostly, she has a passion to just be creative.